I0503173

Prenup Essentials

What Canadians Need To Know

Jeffrey A Behrendt, BA, JD, LLM

DISCLAIMER

This book provides information about the law designed to help readers better understand the legal issues surrounding prenuptial agreements in Canada. But legal information is not the same as legal advice — the application of law to an individual's specific circumstances. Although I am a lawyer, and have done my best to ensure that this information is accurate and useful, you must consult a lawyer if you want professional assurance that this information, and your interpretation of it, is accurate. To clarify further, you may not rely upon this information as legal advice, nor as a recommendation or endorsement of any particular legal understanding.

Copyright 2015 by Jeffrey A Behrendt, BA, JD, LLM

CONTENTS

INTRODUCTION

In the more than 15 years since I was called to the bar, I have seen a dramatic increase in the number of couples that are entering into prenuptial agreements. If you are considering entering into a prenup, then this book is for you.

This book explains, in easy-to-understand terms, what you need to know before entering into a prenuptial agreement. It sets out the legal framework in which prenups operate and explains how a prenup can protect you. It answers that questions I get asked all the time in my legal practice. It details a variety of options that people commonly choose to include in their prenuptial agreements.

What is a Prenuptial Agreement?

A prenuptial agreement is an agreement that sets out what happens financially when your marriage ends. Your marriage will always end – either by separation or eventually death. A prenup goes by a number of names in Canada, including a marriage contract, marriage agreement, marital agreement, interspousal contract, or spousal agreement.

Whether you specifically enter into a prenup or not, the fact is that you are bound by one, namely the rules set out in the Divorce Act, and the family law act and estates act of your province. If you are happy with those rules, then there is no need to enter into a prenuptial agreement. However, most people getting married are unaware of what those rules are, or believe those rules are unfair or do not properly reflect their priorities and values. This book will educate you as to those rules, and help you and your partner decide what to put in your prenup so that it reflects your priorities and values.

What should I put in my Prenuptial Agreement?

The simple answer is whatever you and your partner agree to.

However, that is not really all that helpful, is it? In each chapter I list the most common things I see clients include in their prenups.

Chapter 1: VALIDITY

The first thing most people want to know about prenups is – are they valid? Yes, they are. Well then, why do you hear so many stories about prenuptial agreements being invalidated in court? Two reasons:

(1) Many of these stories are American. The legal situation there is quite different from here in Canada, where many provinces even have specific legislation dealing with prenups.

(2) Not using a lawyer. I know you might think I am biased because I am a lawyer, but I am a big proponent of self-help in the family law area. However, the law regarding prenuptial agreements is an area of law that is too hazardous to go forward without a lawyer even if you and your spouse want a "simple" agreement. That is why this book does not include any templates for you to prepare your own agreement.

Independent Legal Advice

When entering into a prenup, it is important to retain a lawyer to provide you with what is known as "independent legal advice." The lawyer will go through the agreement with you, explain what each of the terms means, ensure that you understand them, answer any questions you have, and make recommendations about any changes that should be made to the agreement.

This independent legal advice offers protection against three typical grounds of attack on a prenuptial agreement:

(1) "**I didn't understand the agreement**." Your spouse may be an educated person with a Master's or even a Ph.D., but if you separate and he or she is not happy

with the prenup, they are going to claim that they did not understand the agreement. This is a difficult claim to dispute – a prenuptial agreement is full of legalese that is difficult to understand. However, if your spouse consulted a lawyer beforehand, then the lawyer has explained the agreement to him or her, and they cannot attack the prenup on this ground.

(2) "**I didn't understand my legal rights**." You may draft your prenup in the plainest English that anyone can understand. However, your spouse can still attack the prenuptial agreement on the ground that he or she did not understand their legal rights. For instance, the prenup may say spousal support is 10% of the payor's income – this is clear and easy to understand. However, if your spouse is not aware of the Spousal Support Advisory Guidelines, and the amount of spousal support they are entitled to pursuant to the Guidelines, then their attack on the agreement will be difficult to defend. By consulting a lawyer, your spouse will be advised about how spousal support works, and what their entitlement to spousal support would be without the prenuptial agreement.

(3) "**I was pressured into signing the agreement**." This becomes a he-said, she-said type of situation where one spouse claims the agreement was entered into voluntarily and the other one claims that he or she was pressured into signing it. Again, using a lawyer prevents such a claim. A lawyer will ask their client whether they are being pressured into signing an agreement, and will sign a certificate stating that there was no such pressure if that is the case.

One Lawyer for Each of You

It would be really efficient if one lawyer could represent both you and your partner, especially if both of you agree on what should go into your prenup. However, the "independent" part of the independent legal advice is important – a lawyer is only permitted to represent one side of the agreement, even if both of you agree on everything. So you will each need a separate lawyer.

Typically, one party's lawyer prepares the agreement, then the other party's lawyer reviews it and suggests changes.

Your partner does not want a lawyer? That may just be a polite way of sabotaging the prenuptial agreement. They are essentially trying to leave open at least three grounds on which to attack the prenup in the future.

If your partner cannot afford a lawyer, you are free to pay for the lawyer on their behalf. Even though you are paying the lawyer, the lawyer will only represent your partner. This is a worthwhile investment to ensure that your prenuptial agreement is valid.

Legal fees are expensive, and ideally you and your partner understand the basics of the legal framework governing prenups. The information in this book is designed to help you do just that. As well, it is helpful if you and your partner agree about what you want your prenup to accomplish prior to consulting with a lawyer, as it can get quite expensive to negotiate a prenuptial agreement through lawyers.

Fairness

A prenuptial agreement does not have to be "fair." However, the reality is it cannot be too one-sided, otherwise a court will invalidate it.

The court's test in Ontario and most other provinces and territories is "unconscionability." If an agreement is unconscionable – that is, it shocks the court's conscience, then a court will invalidate it. In other words, if your prenup gives you a good deal, then it is fine. If it gives you more than just a good deal – let's call it too good a deal – then it may not be upheld in court.

In British Columbia, the standard is whether the prenup is significantly unfair. This is a new standard that was just introduced in 2013, and there is not yet a lot of case law about this in relation to prenuptial agreements. However, it is likely that this standard is a bit lower than that of unconscionability.

Keep in mind that what is fair can vary dramatically depending on the length of your marriage. What is fair in a two-year marriage may be very different from what is fair in a twenty-year marriage. Ideally your prenuptial agreement is flexible enough to deal with both the short run and the long run.

Regardless of the standard, you want to protect your interests, but you do not want to take advantage of your spouse, nor leave them in financial trouble, should your relationship end. If you take advantage of your spouse, the court will intervene and set aside your prenup.

Financial Disclosure
For a prenup to be valid, there must be full financial disclosure. The idea is that you and your partner cannot enter into an agreement dealing with your finances, unless you are aware of the complete financial picture of your partner.

You will need to disclose to your partner your income from all sources, all of your assets and their value, and all of your liabilities and their amounts. This information is then put into a financial statement that becomes part of the prenup.

It is also a good idea to exchange financial disclosure with your partner – that is, exchange documents supporting the figures in your financial statement. This is in case the accuracy of your financial statement is ever challenged in an attempt to invalidate the prenuptial agreement. So, you want to gather up your notices of assessment for the previous three years, a recent pay stub, and bank statements for all of your bank accounts, RRSPs, TFSA, credit cards, lines of credit, and so on. Your partner should do the same, and copies of these documents are exchanged to ensure the accuracy of your financial statement.

For some assets it is not possible to state of a precise value – for instance, the value of your home or car. In these circumstances, an estimate is normally sufficient.

If you own a business, it is usually not necessary to get a formal business appraisal done, but in addition to the documents listed above, you will want to exchange your business' financial statements, tax returns, and notices of assessment for the last three years.

Pensions are a tricky asset and have a different value for family law purposes than the pension plan uses. Again, it is not necessary to have the pension formally valued by an actuary; it is normally sufficient just to disclose its existence.

Subject Matter
There are certain things that one is not permitted to deal with in a prenup; these are covered under the various subject-matter headings of this book. In short, most prenups deal with property division and possibly spousal support; clauses dealing with children and child support are usually not valid.

Fault
I often get requests that there be clauses like "if someone

commits adultery, then they must pay a penalty of …" Clauses dealing with fault are not likely to be enforced. In Canada, all financial issues relating to separation and divorce, such as support and property division, are no fault. This means that they are based solely on economic considerations and not who is at fault in the breakdown of the marriage. The idea is that the breakdown of a marriage is complex and it is normally both parties' fault that a relationship has failed. Also, realistically, a judge does not want to hear all the gory details about who did what to whom in figuring out how to divide a couple's property.

Timing

Timing is a complex issue. In short, the earlier you can enter into a prenup, the better. Ideally, you would enter into your prenuptial agreement at least three months prior to your wedding.

There are no rules in Canada about a minimum amount of time in advance of a wedding by which a prenup must be signed. However, it is not a good idea to wait until the night before the wedding to sign your agreement. This is because one spouse can later argue that there was duress – if they did not sign the agreement, the wedding was cancelled, and everything had already been booked and paid for, all the guests had arrived in town, and so on. A lot of lawyers will not get involved with a prenup if it will not be signed at least one month in advance of the wedding.

That being said, you can even enter into a prenup after your wedding day (this is known as a postnuptial agreement or postnup). Of course waiting until after your wedding day can be a risky proposition – if one party decides not to sign the agreement at that point, it can be a difficult issue with which to deal. However, if you are confident that your partner will sign the agreement, sometimes it is best to wait until after your wedding to sign it, rather than sign it in the few days beforehand. The idea here is to remove any appearance that the agreement was entered into under duress.

Formalities

There are a few other formalities that are necessary for a prenup to be valid. The first is that it must be in writing. So, no matter what your partner promises you, if it is not in your written prenuptial agreement, it is not enforceable in court.

A prenup must be signed and witnessed. The witness can be any adult of sound mind, so a friend, family member, or colleague can be a witness. The witness does not need to read the agreement; they are just confirming that they say you sign the agreement. A prenuptial agreement does not get notarized.

It is a good idea for each party to initial every page of the agreement; this is to prevent pages from being switched out for new pages.

Chapter 2: CUSTODY AND ACCESS

What is Custody and Access?
Custody and access relate to children. Custody is the right to make the important decisions in your child's life, such as health care decisions, educational decisions, and religious decisions. Access is the right to spend time with your child – it is essentially the schedule the children follow as to which parent's home they reside in.

What is the Law regarding Custody and Access?
Custody and access are always decided in a child's best interests. This is a pretty malleable standard that can mean different things to different people. Under section 24(2) of Ontario's Children's Law Reform Act, the following factors are considered:

(a)   the love, affection and emotional ties between the child and,
(i)   each person entitled to or claiming custody of or access to the child,
(ii)   other members of the child's family who reside with the child, and
(iii)   persons involved in the child's care and upbringing;
(b)   the child's views and preferences, if they can reasonably be ascertained;
(c)   the length of time the child has lived in a stable home environment;
(d)   the ability and willingness of each person applying for custody of the child to provide the child with guidance and education, the necessaries of life and any special needs of the child;
(e)   the plan proposed by each person applying for custody of or access to the child for the child's care and upbringing;
(f)   the permanence and stability of the family unit with which it is proposed that the child will live;
(g)   the ability of each person applying for custody of or access to the child to act as a parent; and
(h)   the relationship by blood or through an adoption order between the child and each person who is a party to the application.

Each province and territory has their own legislation, but considerations are pretty much the same everywhere.

Custody and Access in a Prenuptial Agreement
The law is clear that a prenup should not deal with custody and access to children. The idea behind this is that parents cannot know in advance what is in their children's best interests.

There are some exceptions to this, namely that one is permitted to "direct the education and moral training of their children" in a prenuptial agreement.

Given the limited scope for dealing with custody and access in a prenuptial agreement, people don't normally deal with this. However, there are some types of clauses you can put in that deal with children.

OPTION: Cultural heritage
You can put in your prenup that you and spouse intend to educate your children about a particular cultural heritage (or even language). Or you can put in that your children will have a Bar/Bat Mitzvah or similar milestone.

OPTION: Private school
Your prenuptial agreement can state that it is your intention to send your children to a private school (obviously, depending on finances and your children meeting the school's admission criteria).

OPTION: Post-secondary education
Your prenup can state that you intend to send your children to college or university (again, depending on your finances and your children's abilities).

OPTION: No permanent removal from jurisdiction
Where parents are from different places, you may want to make it clear that no child shall be permanently removed from the municipality without the written consent of the other parent.

Chapter 3: CHILD SUPPORT

What is Child Support?

If you and your child's other parent do not live together, there is an automatic obligation for one parent to pay the other child support. If a child resides primarily with one parent, the other parent will be the one to pay child support. Even if a child resides equally with both parents, the higher-income parent will normally pay child support to the lower-income parent.

What is the Law regarding Child Support?

The amount of child support one is required to pay is based on tables that are part of the Child Support Guidelines. You can find a handy online calculator at:

http://www.justice.gc.ca/eng/fl-df/child-enfant/look-rech.asp

So, someone in Ontario earning $75,000 per year with two children is required to pay $1,105 per month in child support. Note that this amount is NOT tax deductible – so it is paid in after tax dollars.

In addition to the table amount of child support, a parent is expected to contribute to what are known as special or extraordinary expenses. Examples of this are orthodontist expenses, private school, before and after school care, expensive extracurricular activities, and so on. These expenses are shared in proportion to the parents' income. So, if you are earning $75,000 per year, and the other parent is earning $25,000 per year, in addition to the table amount of child support, you are required to pay 75% of all your children's special or extraordinary expenses.

Child Support and a New Marriage

One question I often get asked is will the amount of child support I pay go up because I am marrying? The answer is no (except in unusual circumstances, such as your child support having been reduced due to undue hardship).

Child Support in a Prenuptial Agreement

The main principle to keep in mind regarding child support is that a court is free to disregard any provision in a prenup relating to child support. In short, you can put whatever you want about child support into a prenup, but it is almost certain that it will not be enforceable in court. The idea behind this is that child support is the right of the child, and the child is not a party to the prenuptial agreement.

This principle makes a lot of sense in a traditional situation where a young couple is getting married and plan to have children in the future. However, a large percentage of people entering into prenups are marrying for a second time, and already have children from a previous relationship. What most people do not realize is that step-parents can be liable for child support. This is true even if the biological parent is paying child support. So, for instance, a mother can obtain child support from both the biological father, and a step father.

Step-Parents and Child Support

The test to determine whether a stepparent must pay child support is whether the stepparent has stood "in the place of a parent for the child" or as lawyers often say "in loco parentis." Generally, if you have lived with a child for any substantial amount of time, you may well have a liability for child support. However, if you had a more transient relationship, then you may not need to pay child support.

Even if your relationship with the stepchildren is strained, has broken off, or was never very strong, or even if it was the reason for you breaking up with your partner, you may well be found to have acted in loco parentis to the children. This is particularly so if you financially supported the children beforehand, even in an indirect way such as making mortgage payments.

The amount of child support a step-parent is required to pay is at the court's discretion – there are no tables for this, as in the ordinary child support situation. One commonly applied "rule of thumb" is to calculate how much the stepparent would be required to pay under the Child Support Guidelines, then deduct from that the amount of child support that the biological parent is paying.

If the biological parent is not paying anything (for instance, the biological parent is unemployed, ill or cannot be located), then the stepparent may be responsible for paying the full table amount of child support. A stepparent, then, may be required to pay any amount ranging from a token top-up amount to the full amount called for by the Child Support Guidelines.

StepParents and Prenuptial Agreements
I often get asked by people to put provisions in their prenuptial agreements that state that they won't have any responsibility to pay child support for their step-children. As with child support in the traditional situation, the court is free to disregard such provisions. Again, child support is the right of the step-children, and the step-children are not a party to the prenup.

It can still make sense for stepparents to include these provisions in their prenups. It does offer some evidence that the step-parent did not intend to act in loco parentis to the step-children. As well, even if the provision is not legally binding, it may well be morally persuasive. A lot of people are true to their word, even if a court won't force them to be. So, feel free to include such provisions in your agreement. However, just be aware that if push comes to shove, you may still end up paying child support, regardless of what your prenuptial agreement says.

Chapter 4: SPOUSAL SUPPORT

What is Spousal Support (also known as Alimony, Maintenance, Spousal Maintenance)?

When a couple separates, often the higher income earning spouse will end up paying spousal support to the lower income earning spouse. This is known as spousal support. It is awarded to compensate spouses for the roles they played during the marriage, and any disadvantages they suffer as a result of the marriage ending.

What is the Law regarding Spousal Support?

There are two steps in determining spousal support. The first step is determining whether there is an entitlement to spousal support. If there is an entitlement to spousal support, the next step is determining the amount of spousal support.

Regarding entitlement, the types of things that create an entitlement to spousal support are choices, such as sacrificing your career to raise children, or to accommodate your spouse's career, for instance by moving from city to city, making it difficult to progress in your career, actively working to promote your spouse's career, for instance through regular business entertaining, and so on. However, the reality is that in most longer relationships, particularly where there is a large income differential between the spouses, a court will find an entitlement to spousal support.

The amount of spousal support awarded is in the court's discretion. There are guidelines, known as the Spousal Support Advisory Guidelines. Unlike the Child Support Guidelines, these are advisory only; courts are not required to follow them. However, realistically, generally the courts do follow them unless there are really exceptional circumstances.

The Guidelines also provide a range of support, and usually the argument between spouses is whether support should be paid at the high or low end of the range. A court will decide where in the range given by the Guidelines, based on a number of factors, such as your income, your spouse's income, your health, your spouse's health, the roles each of you played during the marriage, and so on.

Spousal support is tax deductible; so your actual out-of-pocket cost of paying spousal support is less than the amount you are paying.

You can find an online spousal support calculator at: http://www.mysupportcalculator.ca/Calculator.aspx

If you play around with the calculator, you will note that spousal support payments are surprisingly high. For example, if you earn $100,000 and your spouse is a stay-at-home parent with two children, you will pay child support of $1,416 per month, plus most of the children's special or extraordinary expenses, plus between $1,226 and $1,722 per month in spousal support. When you take taxes, CPP deductions, and EI deductions into account, you will only be left with a bit more than $40,000 per year after paying child support and the high range of spousal support.

The length of time spousal support is payable depends on whether there are children. The minimum length of time spousal support is payable is half the length of the marriage. So, if you were married for 10 years, spousal support would be payable for at least 5 years. If there are no children, spousal support generally ends no later than the number of years your marriage lasted. So, for a 10-year marriage, you would pay spousal support for up to 10 years. For a marriage with children, spousal support could go even long – until the children all finish their first post-secondary degree. What's more, a court is often loathe to predict when you will no longer need to pay spousal support, so for long-term marriages, spousal support will generally be indefinite. Indefinite means that the court does not set an end date – you will need to go back to court in the future to try to stop spousal support.

Spousal Support and a New Marriage

Will your new marriage effect the amount of spousal support you pay or receive? Quite possibly. At the very least, a new marriage by a spousal support payor or recipient will likely be grounds for review of spousal support. This question is too fact specific to know for sure in advance – you will realistically need to spend an hour or so with a lawyer reviewing the details of your situation.

If you are a spousal support recipient, there is no automatic presumption that just because you are getting married, your spousal support will end or be reduced. However, you may have entered into a separation agreement that states this will happen. If that is not the case, it is going to depend on the reason you are receiving spousal support. If it is to compensate you for career losses during your relationship, then your new marriage is not likely to affect your spousal support. If you are receiving spousal support because of a need for support, your need for support may well be reduced because of your new marriage, in which case spousal support may well be reduced.

If you are a spousal support payor, it is possible that spousal support will go up if you marry. This will happen if the amount of spousal support you were paying was limited by your financial ability, but was not the amount needed by the support recipient or required to compensate for career losses.

Immigration and Spousal Support

If you plan on sponsoring your partner to live in Canada once you get married, you will sign an undertaking with the Federal government that you will support your spouse for three years. This is an agreement between you and the government. As the government is not a party to your prenup, nothing you put in your prenuptial agreement can override this.

Spousal Support in a Prenuptial Agreement

You can deal with spousal support in your prenup, but you have to be careful what you put in your agreement. A court is going to scrutinize closely the spousal support provisions of a prenup. As discussed in the chapter on validity, if a court finds them unconscionable (or grossly unfair in British Columbia), then the court will invalidate them. A stereotypical example of this would be if one spouse is going to need social assistance due to the spousal support provisions in the prenup. This would normally be considered unconscionable and spousal support would be awarded, regardless of what the prenuptial agreement said.

Note that if you are a high income earner and your spouse is not, then you are going to need to be careful about limiting spousal support, particularly if your relationship lasts any length of time.

When you are deciding what to put into your agreement regarding spousal support, you need to think carefully about all of the vagaries of life. Simply because you and your spouse are doing well financially now does not mean that will always be the case. In particular, you should consider: what happens if one of you become unemployed and unable to find a new job, what happens if you have children, what happens if one of you becomes disabled, what happens on retirement, what happens if one of you needs to give up a job to accommodate the other's career, and so on.

Here are some options you can consider:

OPTION: Don't put anything in regarding spousal support
If you do not put anything in your prenup regarding spousal support, the regular rules of spousal support will apply. This is a perfect option for the traditional younger couple who plan on having children together. Given that neither of you is likely to be established in your careers yet, you will be having children, and you could be together a very long time, it can be difficult to predict what will happen in the future. Simply being silent on the issue is likely your best bet in these circumstances.

OPTION: Complete spousal support release
This option basically means that no matter what happens, no spousal support will ever be payable by either party. This may be appropriate in situation where a couple is older, does not plan to have children, and are established financially.

OPTION: Partial spousal support release
This option basically means that no spousal support is payable except in circumstances that are set out in the prenuptial agreement. Examples of these circumstances may be one party becoming disabled, or the couple having children.

OPTION: Low range of the Spousal Support Advisory Guidelines
As discussed previously, the Spousal Support Advisory Guidelines don't provide a single number for the amount of spousal support; instead they provide a range. The idea behind this option is that the low end of the range is chosen. The advantage of this is that it is flexible enough to

accommodate pretty much whatever happens in the future. As well, it is very unlikely to be found unconscionable by a court, and thus invalid, as the amount of spousal support payable will be within the range set out by the Guidelines.

OPTION: Your own formula for spousal support
Don't like the amount set out in the Spousal Support Advisory Guidelines? You can create your own formula to deal with the uniqueness of your own situation. Many couples come to me with their own formula, often based on a percentage of what the higher income earner earns, or a percentage of the difference between their two incomes.

OPTION: Fixed amount
You either pay a certain lump sum amount or a fixed amount each month if your marriage ends. In determining this amount, you should take inflation into account, and perhaps even index this amount to the Consumer Price Index. Also note that unlike monthly spousal support, lump sum spousal support is not tax deductible by the payor or taxable in the hands of the recipient.

OPTION: Different amounts based on the length of the marriage
A certain amount will be payable if the marriage is less than, for instance, two years, a higher amount will be payable if the marriage lasts, for example, from two to five years, and a higher amount still will be paid the longer the marriage is.

OPTION: Time limited
If you are not happy with how long spousal support is payable under the Spousal Support Advisory Guidelines, you can set out in your prenup how long you agree that it should be payable.

OPTION: Specific purpose

You can limit spousal support in your prenuptial agreement so that it will only be paid for a specific purpose, for instance, so that one party can obtain a degree, or get retrained for a new job.

OPTION: No compensation for something

You can state in your prenup that there will be no compensation for a particular choice made by a party. For instance, if your partner gives up a job to move to your city when you get married, you can state that there will be no compensation for this.

OPTION: Disability insurance required

If your spouse is disabled and unable to earn an income, spousal support payments are likely, regardless of what your prenup says. One way to protect yourself against this is to require each spouse to carry disability insurance.

OPTION: Income from certain sources not considered for spousal support

Perhaps you receive income from rental properties you own, or are the beneficiary of a trust when you get married. In this scenario, you may not want to pay spousal support based on these income streams, especially as they existed prior to marriage. A prenup can exclude income sources from being considered in determining the amount of spousal support. In doing this, you need to be careful that you are not excluding so much that the spousal support provisions would be considered unconscionable by a court.

What is Property?

Under family law, property has a very extensive definition. Basically, it means not just real estate, but any and all assets.

What is the Law regarding Division of Property?

Under the Constitution, property is a provincial matter. So each province and territory has its own property division regime. The regimes are very similar in their general principles; however, the details vary from province to province.

Ontario

In Ontario, the increase in value of assets of both parties during the marriage is shared, (with the exception of certain assets, discussed below). If you want to get into the nitty gritty of the calculation, add together the value of all of your assets, deduct from this value of all of your debts, deduct from this the value of all of your assets on the date of marriage, and add to this the value all of your debts on your date of marriage. This gives you your "net family property." Do the same for your spouse.

Then an "equalization payment" is made. The amount of the equalization payment is half the difference between your and your spouse's net family property. So, after the equalization payment, you should both have the same net family property. For instance, if your net family property is $100,000 and your spouse's net family property is $50,000, you would make an equalization payment of $25,000 to your spouse, so that you are each left with $75,000.

Note that it is the value of the assets that is divided, and not the assets themselves.

As mentioned above, certain assets are excluded from the calculation of your net family property, namely inheritances, gifts from third parties, proceeds of life insurance policies, and personal injury awards, <u>so long as you don't put these monies into a matrimonial home</u>. The part about not putting the money into a matrimonial home is important. A lot of people when they receive a substantial amount of money, use that to buy a home or upgrade a home.

British Columbia

In British Columbia, all "family property" is divided equally between the spouses. Property excluded from family property includes property owned before marriage, inheritances, gifts from third parties, personal injury awards, proceeds of life insurance policies, and beneficial interests in discretionary trusts in certain cases. The increase in value of excluded property is included in family property.

Alberta

In Alberta, all "matrimonial property" is divided equally between the spouses. Matrimonial property is all property acquired by the spouses during the marriage except for inheritances, gifts from third parties, and personal injury awards. Other property is considered exempt property, and not divided. However, the increase in value assets owned on the date of marriage must be shared in a just and equitable manner.

Saskatchewan

In Saskatchewan, all "family property" is divided equally. Property acquired before marriage is exempt, as well as personal injury awards, proceeds of life insurance policies, but not increases in their value during the marriage.

Manitoba

In Manitoba, each spouse values all their assets on the date of separation. The spouse with the greater net worth then pays half the difference in net worth to the other spouse. Jointly owned assets are not covered. Gifts and inheritances are exempt from division. Assets owned at the date of marriage are exempt from division, but any increase in their value is not.

Nova Scotia

Matrimonial property is divided equally between the spouses. This includes all property except third-party gifts, inheritances, personal injury awards, proceeds of life insurance policies, personal items, and business assets.

New Brunswick

In New Brunswick, "marital property" is shared equally between spouses. Marital property includes all property except certain business property, inheritances, third-party gifts, and inheritances.

Newfoundland

In Newfoundland, "matrimonial assets" are divided equally between spouses. Matrimonial assets include all property except third-party gifts, inheritances, family heirlooms, personal injury awards, and businesses.

Prince Edward Island

In Prince Edward Island, each party calculates what their property is worth. An equalization payment of half the difference in net values is made by the spouse with the higher net value to the other spouse.

Yukon

In Yukon, each spouse gets half of all family assets. Most assets are considered family assets, regardless of whether they were acquired before or after marriage. Personal items such as clothing are not considered family assets, nor are businesses where only one spouse was involved considered family assets.

Northwest Territories
In Northwest Territories, the parties' family property is divided equally, except for assets and debts brought into the marriage, proceeds of a life insurance policy, and personal injury awards. A payment is made from the spouse with the higher family property to the other spouse to equalize family property.

Nunavut
In Nunavut, the parties' family property is divided equally, except for assets and debts brought into the marriage, proceeds of a life insurance policy, and personal injury awards. A payment is made from the spouse with the higher family property to the other spouse to equalize family property.

Property Division in a Prenuptial Agreement
For most people this is the heart of the prenuptial agreement. So long as you and your partner agree on it, you can put pretty much anything about property division that you want into a prenup (so long as it is not unconscionable). You can deal with currently owned assets, and assets that are acquired during the marriage. You can be as creative as you want and tailor things to your situation as much as you want. Here are some typical scenarios I see in my practice.

OPTION: Separate as to property
This property regime is what most people think of when they think of a prenup – what is mine is mine, and what is your is yours. Ownership is determined by title. If something is jointly owned, it is shared between the parties. Throughout your marriage you can control exactly who gets through title. For instance, if you want a cottage shared 60/40, simply ensure

one of you owns 60% of the cottage, and the other owns 40% of the cottage. This property regime works well for older couples who are already established financially, have good careers, and do not plan on having children.

OPTION: Certain assets not divided
Under this option, a couple will divide their assets the same as if they did not have a prenup. However, some assets are excluded from this division of property, for instance, a home, a pension, or a business. This is the option most people are thinking of when they say "I want to protect my 'xyz' in a prenup."

OPTION: Set out date of marriage assets
Under this option, assets are divided in the same way as they would be without a prenuptial agreement; however, the value of the date of marriage assets is specified. If you recall our discussion above, in most provinces and territories, the value of assets brought into a marriage are not divided. However, the reality is if you marriage lasts 10 or 20 years, it can be difficult to recall exactly what you owned on the date of marriage, much less come up with documentary proof for it. Many divorces involve people squabbling about what they brought into the marriage. This sort of a provision ensures that you really get credit for what you owned on the date of marriage, regardless of how much time has passed, how much memories fade, and how difficult it is to locate bank statements from years ago.

OPTION: Property divided as in another jurisdiction
I see this option chosen a lot by immigrants. For instance, the couple comes from Germany, and wants their property treated as it would be if they were governed by German family law.

OPTION: Protect inheritances and gifts

Say that you will be receiving $100,000 from your parents, and want to use that money to buy a matrimonial home. If you did not buy the home, this money would not be subject to property division, but by buying a matrimonial home, it is. A prenup can ensure that even if you put inheritances or gifts from third parties into a home, those funds will not be subject to property division.

OPTION: Protect yourself from your partner's debts

Your partner is not the best at managing money, and routinely runs up large debts. Even without a prenup, you will not be directly responsible for these debts. However, they can dramatically increase your equalization payment to your partner, but reducing your partner's net worth. A prenup can exclude certain debts from being used in calculating the equalization payment.

OPTION: Dealing with a business

If only one spouse owns a business, and the other one is not involved in the business, then you can deal with the business as you would any other asset. However, if you and your spouse are both involved in the business, particularly if both of you have an ownership interest, then your prenuptial agreement should set out what happens to the business if your relationship ends, ideally providing a mechanism for one partner to buy the other partner out.

Chapter 6: MATRIMONIAL HOME

What is a Matrimonial Home?
The matrimonial home is the home you and your spouse live in.

There can be more than one matrimonial home. For instance, if you and your spouse live in one home for the winter and another home for the summer, both may be matrimonial homes. Or, if you spend most of your time living in a home, and your spouse spends most of their time living in the cottage, both the home and the cottage may be matrimonial homes.

What is the Law regarding Matrimonial Homes?
Matrimonial homes are given special treatment under the law. The idea is that a home is a special kind of asset, with more than just monetary value, as it is where you live.

Even if you own the matrimonial home, you cannot kick your spouse out of the home. Nor can you sell it, transfer it, rent it, or mortgage it without your spouse's permission.

In addition to this, in Ontario, the matrimonial home is treated differently when it comes to property division. If you bring an asset into the marriage, say $100,000 in cash, then when you separate, you get credit for bringing that asset into the marriage. However, if that same $100,000 was instead $100,000 of equity in a matrimonial home, and you are still living in that same home on the date of separation, you would NOT get credit for bringing that asset into the marriage (except perhaps if the relationship lasts for less than 5 years). So, in both cases, you are entering into the marriage with the same amount of money, but in one case, because the money was invested in a home, you get a substantially worse result on separation.

Matrimonial Home in a Prenuptial Agreement

A lot of people come to me with the impression that they cannot deal with the matrimonial home in a prenup. This is not quite true. You CAN deal with ownership of the matrimonial home. However, you CANNOT set out who will leave the home if you separate. Nor can the non-owning spouse release the requirement that they give permission before a matrimonial home can be sold, transferred, rented, or mortgaged.

A lot of people enter into prenuptial agreement just to deal with their homes, as that is their major asset. As well, a lot of people in Ontario believe that the special treatment of the matrimonial home in property division is unfair, and enter into a prenup just because of that.

Matrimonial Home Options

In a prenup, you can treat your matrimonial home the same as all of your other assets, or you can single it out and treat it differently. You can be as creative as you want in your treatment of the home. To get you started, here are some typical types of arrangements I've seen:

OPTION: Credit for bringing the matrimonial home into the marriage (Ontario only)
Your prenup can state that the matrimonial home is treated like any other asset brought into the marriage. So, if the matrimonial home has $100,000 of equity in it when you get married, you would get credit for bringing $100,000 into the marriage, as if it were cash or any other asset.

Note: an alternative to entering into a prenuptial agreement that does this is simply to sell your home after you get married, but before you separate.

OPTION: Matrimonial home always belongs to one party
Another common way people deal with matrimonial homes in their prenuptial agreements is to state that no matter what happens, the matrimonial home will always belong to the owner. In other words, it is completely excluded from any division of property. Many people have worked hard their entire lives so that they can own a home; they don't want to lose half of it if their marriage goes south.

Note that, as discussed above, just because you own the matrimonial home, does not mean you can kick your spouse out, or that you can sell, transfer, rent, or mortgage your home.

OPTION: Interest in home obtained through marriage
The idea here is that the longer the marriage, the larger the interest that the originally non-owning spouse gets. A typical example of this is one spouse obtaining a 2% interest in the home for each year of marriage, until a maximum of 50% is reached. This sort of arrangement is common where one spouse does not work and will not be able to contribute financially to the home.

OPTION: Each spouse gets a certain percentage of the home
Perhaps one spouse paid for 2/3 of the home and the other paid for 1/3 of the home. They are sharing expenses related to the upkeep of the home 2/3 and 1/3. Then the home is divided 2/3 and 1/3. Alternatively, perhaps one party put $100,000 down and the other party put $50,000 down into the original payment for the house. Each party gets their downpayment

back, then the remainder of the equity in the house is shared equally when the home is sold or the relationship ends.

OPTION: One spouse gets credit for all contributions made to home
In this situation, one spouse owns the home, but sometimes the other will make financial contributions to the home. The prenup requires that these contributions are kept track of, and reimbursed (sometimes with interest) when the home is sold or the relationship ends.

OPTION: House divided according to contributions
If you and your partner are scrupulous about keeping records, then you can agree to share the matrimonial home according to how much money each party has contributed. Basically, each of you would be reimbursed for any contributions made, and any increase in the home's equity would be shared.

NOT AN OPTION: Possession of home
You cannot include a clause in your prenup that requires your spouse to leave the matrimonial home if you separate.

Chapter 7: ESTATES

Estates and Marriage

Traditionally, in provinces and territories other than Quebec, a will became invalid on marriage. The idea behind this is that an old will may not take into account your new spouse, so many people may inadvertently cut their spouses out of their estate.

New legislation has recently been introduced in Alberta and British Columbia so that this is no longer the case in those two provinces. It is still the case in all other provinces and territories (except Quebec) that a will becomes invalid on marriage.

It is a good idea to make a new will when you are about to get married, even in provinces where this is not required. Creating a new will is often done in conjunction with a creating a prenup, as there is an overlap between the issues dealt with in each legal document.

What is the Law regarding Estates?

No Will

If you pass away without a will, that is known in legal jargon as passing away "intestate." There are specific rules about what happens to a person's property if he or she passes away intestate. Under the Constitution, property is a provincial matter, so each province has its own rules. The intestacy rules for each province are as follows.

In all provinces except Quebec, if you don't have a will, are married, and there are no children, then your spouse inherits everything.

If you don't have a will, are married, and have children, then generally your spouse gets a preferential portion of your estate, and the balance is divided between your spouse and each of your children.

In Ontario, the preferential portion of your estate that goes to your spouse is $200,000, while in British Columbia it is $300,000, in Alberta it is $150,000, in Saskatchewan it is $100,000, in Nova Scotia it is $50,000, in New Brunswick it is the marital property (see the property division of this book for more details), in Newfoundland it is $0, in Prince Edward Island it is $0, in Northwest Territories it is $50,000, in Yukon it is $75,000, and in Nunavut it is $50,000.

In these provinces, if you are married with one child, the remainder of your estate is split equally between your spouse and child. In these provinces, if you are married with more than one child, then one-third of the remainder of your estate goes to your spouse, and the other two-thirds are split equally between your children.

For example, if you live in Ontario, are married with two children and your estate is worth $500,000, the first $200,000 goes to your spouse, and of the remaining $300,000, $100,000 goes to your spouse, $100,000 goes to your first child, and $100,000 goes to you second child.

In Manitoba, even if you and your spouse have children, if you do not have a will, your estate passes entirely to your spouse.

The Matrimonial Home
Some provinces and territories have special rules regarding inheriting the matrimonial home. In Nova Scotia, Northwest Territories, and Nunavut, a spouse may elect to keep the matrimonial home instead of taking their preferential share, or if the home is worth less than the preferential share, a spouse

can elect to keep the matrimonial home as part of their preferential share.

As well, there are rules regarding possession of the matrimonial home. For instance, in Ontario the surviving spouse can stay in the home for a period of 60 days following the other spouse's death.

But wait…
That's not all! Whether you pass away intestate or leave a will, your spouse may have an option to make a matrimonial claim on your estate. The idea behind this is that you cannot simply cut your spouse and children out of your inheritance through a will.

All provinces and territories except British Columbia, Prince Edward Island, and Yukon have legislation setting out minimum amounts of property that your spouse must receive. In these provinces and territories, the surviving spouse can elect to receive the same amount that he or she would have received if the two of you had separated on the day the other spouse passed away. You can review the property division section of this book to get the precise details. However, even in British Columbia, Prince Edward Island, and Yukon, there are remedies available for a spouse dissatisfied with what was left to him or her.

There's more…
Your spouse may also be entitled to receive what is known as dependant's relief. The idea behind this is similar to spousal support – it is support so that your spouse can continue to support himself or herself adequately.

Estates in a Prenuptial Agreement
A lot of people do not realize that a prenup can also be an

estate planning tool. A prenuptial agreement comes into effect when a relationship ends – this can either be by separation or by one party passing away. So, while a prenuptial agreement is not a substitute for a will, it can set out minimum requirements for wills or release parties from legislated obligations on their estate.

The most common scenario where this is handy is when one or both partners have children from a previous relationship. In that situation, you may want your estate to go completely or primarily to your children from the previous relationship, rather than to your new spouse. As discussed above, you cannot simply create a will that cuts your new spouse out. However, you can get around this by agreeing in a prenup. For instance, you can agree with your partner that your estates are under no financial obligations to each other, or that you will not make a matrimonial claim on each other's estates.

Estate Options
Like property division, you can put pretty much anything into your prenup about what will happen to your estate, so long as you and your partner agree to it.

Option: Do nothing
If you do not put anything in your prenup about your estate, then all the regular rules regarding estates apply. This is a good option if you and your partner are entering a traditional first marriage, or even if you and your partner are not sure what you want to do with your estate.

Generally, people are willing to be more generous to their spouse if their spouse has stayed with them until they passed away, then if the relationship ends in a separation. So, this option is often a good one.

Option: Complete release

This means that neither you nor your spouse are required to leave each other anything or support the other after one of you passes away. This is appropriate for older, financially established couples, particularly if one or both of them have children from a previous relationship.

Option: Minimum requirements

Your prenup can require that you and your spouse each leave the other a certain minimum amount of money or other assets. This guarantees a certain standard of living for the surviving spouse, yet allows you more flexibility in dealing with your remaining assets.

Option: No matrimonial claim

As discussed above, legislation in most provinces gives your spouse an option to make a matrimonial claim against your assets, normally for the amount that they would inherit if you had separated on the day you passed away. This can be waived in a prenup, allowing you more flexibility in determining how to plan your estate.

Option: Matrimonial home

A house is often a couple's main asset. You may wish to require that your spouse leaves you the house if he or she passes away, or at least lets you stay there for the rest of your life.

Option: Life insurance

Often people have life insurance through employment that is a certain multiple of their income, or they may own other life insurance policies. A prenup can require that these policies designate the other spouse as the beneficiary. A prenup can even require a spouse to obtain a policy for your benefit.

Option: Pensions

Often pensions have survivor benefits. Like life insurance, a prenup can require that your spouse designate you as the beneficiary of the pension survivor benefits.

Chapter 8: JURISDICTIONAL ISSUES

What is Jurisdiction?
In legal terms, jurisdiction refers to a geographic area and the law that applies in that area. So, Ontario is a jurisdiction, and Ontario law applies within that jurisdiction.

What is the Law regarding Jurisdiction?
The court where the defendant resides has jurisdiction over the defendant (the defendant is the person being sued). The court where property is located has jurisdiction over that property. The court where the children are living will have jurisdiction over issues relating to the children.

Normally, it will be obvious which jurisdiction to proceed in – it is where you and your partner are living. So, if you lived together in Vancouver, and separate there, then the law of British Columbia applies.

Note also that the jurisdiction in which you get married does not matter. So, if you go to the Caribbean for a destination wedding, or get married back home in another province so your family can attend, that does not change the law that applies to your family law matter.

Similarly, citizenship or nationality of a spouse has no bearing on family law jurisdiction in Canada.

Jurisdiction in a Prenuptial Agreement
If you and your partner live in a particular province, and plan to spend the rest of your lives in that province, then jurisdiction is not an issue for you, and you can skip this chapter. However, nowadays people are more mobile, so the issue of jurisdiction is important.

If you and your partner live in different provinces, you will want to get a prenuptial agreement prepared in the province that you are going to be living in when you marry. For example, if you live in Toronto, and your partner lives in Vancouver, and when you marry your partner will join you in Toronto, you will want to get an Ontario prenup.

If you have a prenup in one province, and end up moving to another province (other than possibly Quebec; the law there is very different and you would need to consult with a Quebec lawyer), that will normally be fine. An Alberta court will normally uphold a Saskatchewan prenuptial agreement, and apply Saskatchewan law to its interpretation.

Prenups become problematic, however, if you end up living in a jurisdiction outside of Canada. There is no guarantee that a foreign court, for instance a Florida or an English court, will uphold your agreement, regardless of what you put in your agreement. (Similarly, Canadian courts often do not uphold foreign prenuptial agreements). The reason for this is that family law differs dramatically from country to country, and the chances that a prenuptial agreement in one country will meet the requirements of a prenuptial agreement in another country are slim. This is so even if you have a clause in your agreement stating that it is to be interpreted, for example, under Ontario law by an Ontario court.

If you know that it is very likely that you will be living in another country during your marriage, or even if it is a strong possibility that one spouse would move to another country if your marriage ended, it is strongly advised that you enter into a prenup in that other country as well. This would be a "mirror" prenup – the same as your Canadian prenuptial agreement, but valid under the law of the foreign jurisdiction. You will need to work closely with lawyers in both jurisdictions to ensure that both prenuptial agreements are valid, and that one prenup does not invalidate the other.

CONCLUSION

One thing that most people do not realize is that a prenup does not need to be forever. You can set a time limit in the agreement after which the agreement, or part of it, expires.

Prenuptial agreements can also be flexible. Provided that you and your spouse agree on a change, you and your spouse can change a prenup at any time, or even cancel the agreement altogether.

There is also something known as a review clause that you can include in a prenuptial agreement. Basically this clause states that after a certain number of years, say five or ten years, you and your spouse will review what is in the agreement to determine whether it still makes sense. If it does not, then the two of you will decide how the agreement should be amended.

These are the basics of prenuptial agreements in Canada. If, after reading this book, you have any questions, I am always happy to hear from you. You can reach me via email through my website at Prenup.ca.

www.ingramcontent.com/pod-product-compliance
Lightning Source LLC
Chambersburg PA
CBHW071011180526
45168CB00003B/1374